THE GREAT FALL

Principles to Fall into a Successful Career and Life

BY

Shameka Guffie

The Great Fall: Principles to Fall into a Successful Career and Life

Copyright © 2020 by Shameka Guffie. All rights reserved.

First Edition

ISBN 978-1-7355042-0-9

PO Box 11712, Houston, TX 77293

Brief news excerpts, public statements, and images by individuals or companies other than the author are used under section 107 of the copyright act 1976; allowance is made for "fair use" for purposes such as criticism, commentary, news reporting, teaching, scholarship, and research.

No part of this book may be reproduced in whole or in part, stored in a retrieval system, or transmitted in any form, or by any means, electronic, mechanical, photocopying, recording, or otherwise, without prior permission of the author, except by a reviewer, who may quote brief passages in a review.

All Scripture quotation, unless otherwise indicated, are taken from the Holy Bible, King James Version®. KJV®. Copyright © 1973, 1978, 1984 by International Bible Society. Used by permission of Zondervan Publishing House. All rights reserved.

https://www.kingjamesbibleonline.org/Ephesians-6-12

Table of Contents

The Cause

Chapter 1

Falling Into An Intentional Life 15

Chapter 2

Comfortability, A Common Choice 21

Chapter 3

You Versus Comfortability 31

Chapter 4

Delays Due To Contingencies 53

Chapter 5

The Results From Rushing 63

The Stumble

Chapter 6

Focus, A Necessity 73

Chapter 7

Consistent Until The End 81

The Fall

Chapter 8

Going Down 87

The Audience

Chapter 9

There Is Always Someone Watching 101

Chapter 10

Audience Member 1: The Non-Reactor 103

Chapter 11

Audience Member 2: The Promoter 109

Chapter 12

Audience Member 3: The Excuser 113

Chapter 13

Audience Member 4: You 117

Vision From The Ground

Chapter 14

Turn Opposition Into Opportunity 123

Chapter 15

Renewal Of The Mind 129

Chapter 16

Inspiration To Live, My Way 135

About Author 139

DEDICATION

This book is dedicated to Louise Lee, a strong woman who raised seven children and eighteen grandchildren. Despite the large number of family members, she intentionally made every person feel as if they were "her favorite." Until she took her last breath, she poured hope, love, independence, honor, education, and faith into every one of us.

THE CAUSE

CHAPTER 1

FALLING INTO AN INTENTIONAL LIFE

Before New Year's Day in 2018, had anyone asked me what greatness I was to achieve, I would not have been able to answer. I could have mentioned all the ideas I have considered in the past, but I had no clear direction. Therefore, I ended 2017 with overflowing passion, to do, well, nothing. I was full of excitement and sure of possibilities but had no clear path to take.

I was 33 years old, and by my standards, I was a successful accountant. I made enough money to afford some luxuries that life offers or at least the items in which I had an interest. My family and I lived in a lovely house, drove good cars, and had all our needs met with money left to save.

THE GREAT FALL

Undoubtedly, my career was blossoming. In fact, I had accomplished all the career goals I had set for myself about eight years ago. I was a dedicated employee at my job. I worked overtime, worked from home, answered emails during the middle of the night, and so on. My job responsibilities went with me everywhere. Perhaps the company was the "other" family member since I allocated so much of my time and effort towards them. I was a member of an executive team with hopes to continue growing in the company.

I enjoyed working for my employer and would have been comfortable working there until retirement. I thought this would be my last job, and, like my parents, I would remain an employee for the next twenty-plus years. Although I enjoyed what I was doing and I liked the company, I was often stressed. But isn't everyone?

Despite my life appearing to be on track, I ended 2017 with a new emptiness. There was a void I couldn't satisfy with achievements and status. At that stage in my life, I knew I needed a change. Nevertheless, what do I change? I had no idea. I knew I would do something different. I was destined for more, specifically, greatness. Yet, I had no desire to dream or accomplish new goals. I had no direction. Why should I? From my perspective, life was good.

However, I would soon discover how this first day of a new year came with its message, a powerful and memorable message declared with certainty.

I never knew what was coming. With a divided mind, yet open heart, the year began with an incident. Or rather, an accident that resulted in an instant revelation. The revelation was simple in form but complex in nature. The accident addressed life's challenges. Even, it exposed the secrets to life. The message I received is not new but became apparent on the day I experienced *The Great Fall*.

If you are one of the lucky ones, you can experience life daily. I do not mean waking up in the morning, going to work, commenting on social media, eating,

THE GREAT FALL

watching television, and going to sleep. And then, expecting to repeat this process every day until the day you return to dust. I am referring to taking in stride, bumps, and bruises life exposes you to and appreciating every minute. As you age and gain wisdom, you will realize your experiences have a purpose.

Therefore, I encourage you to live intentionally, using every experience, whether planned or unplanned, in your favor. Unlike other people who believe you need to find your purpose, I believe it has been with you from birth. That is the reason you have specific skills and interests. However, are you living or allowing life to happen? The difference between the two is whether you are an active (living) or passive (allowing life to happen) steward of your life.

You see, I knew my accident occurred to make me cherish my life more. I realized, every moment—including the unfavorable times— was precious, and I could accomplish any vision I had. All options are available, including settling to accept my situation.

FALLING INTO AN INTENTIONAL LIFE

The accident occurred to provide a viable and memorable message for me to live by and to develop wisdom I could share with others. So, I fell.

My fall started with a belt. "A belt?" you ask. Well, my answer is, "Why, yes." You'll get the whole picture soon.

As a mother, I feel obligated to attend to the needs of the other members of the family. I am a mother of three beautiful children who make frequent requests of me daily.

My fall occurred while attempting to fulfill the needs of my oldest son, Peter. While dressing Peter that afternoon for a New Year's gathering, he declared that his pants were too big and that he must have a belt to secure his pants. But Peter's pants were not too big. Peter was a growing boy who had outgrown many of his clothes. The pants he had on were looser than the previous pairs, but not too big. And based on the tan-

THE GREAT FALL

trum Peter was throwing, it was clear he wasn't convinced that the new pants were his size. That day, I learned my first lesson on comfort.

CHAPTER 2

COMFORTABILITY, A COMMON CHOICE

Like Peter, many of us fall into the trap and trickery of comfortability. The pants that Peter preferred to wear were tight and cuffed above his ankles (some may use the term "flooding"). Peter was fighting to wear the tighter-fitting pants because he was accustomed to wearing them. A few days before this incident, I purchased new pants for him after witnessing—on several occasions—the difficulties Peter was having while getting dressed. However, Peter was convinced that the tighter-fitting pants were not only better but were "his favorite" pants. The pants were his favorite, not because they fit around his waist snugly but because Peter grew accustomed to the feeling of the tight fit.

THE GREAT FALL

It was then that I discovered that I was just like my son. I often stay in tight situations because, after so much invested time, I have gained comfort.

In November 2016, I started experiencing daily migraines. I would wake up every morning with excruciating pain in my eyes and head. I did not have a history of migraines. So, after months of agony, some people advised me to visit a neurologist. I chose a doctor who was highly recommended by multiple individuals and had over 25 years of experience as I desired a permanent cure and not just palliative treatment.

Well, after my first visit, the doctor asked me to keep a journal to identify specific triggers that could be causing the migraines. After about eight months of journaling and multiple visits to the neurologist, there were no foods or extracurricular activities linked explicitly as a cause for the daily migraines.

Far from a conclusion, the neurologist asked me to take two weeks of vacation from work. I immediately

COMFORTABILITY, A COMMON CHOICE

requested the time off. After staying away from work for fourteen days, I experienced only one migraine.

If I am honest with myself, I did not need the two-week experiment to determine that my work caused the migraines. Long before writing the journals, I perceived that the job caused the migraines. Yet, I wanted to believe I was wrong.

Factually, there are ten common triggers for migraines, and I was intimate with the top two causes: stress and irregular sleep. As noted, I was always working, even during the night. It was common for me to grab my laptop or my cell phone to read messages from affiliates who worked on the other side of the world. Also, I created an environment that did not include a work-life balance, and I made this extra stress "normal." Due to my elaborate career goals, I accepted the uncommon and made it comfortable. So, when the neurologist concluded that my current job was probably causing the migraines, you would think I would make a change.

THE GREAT FALL

On the contrary, I remained with the company. Familiarity convinced me that the benefits of my current position overshadowed the pain and agony associated with staying. I believed I would grow to accept the "tightness" and convinced myself this was the only option for my life. The job provided financial stability, intellectual challenges, and a successful career path. I have invested years of services, built relationships throughout the company, and was comfortable with my current and future direction. Where would I find similar opportunities?

I could see that Peter was determined to wear his favorite comfortable pants while I knew they didn't fit anymore. In the same way, your loved ones can often see the tightness of your "comfortable" decisions before you can. They will attempt to convince you to try "new pants." However, the comfortability and false security of the "right" decisions are difficult to let go of.

COMFORTABILITY, A COMMON CHOICE

In my case, my husband could see the vast level of stress I was accepting with my constant over-working. However, I allowed my "comfortable" decisions to persuade me that my current situation was best for me. I did not go as far as saying it was my "favorite." However, I included enough reasoning to justify my choice to stay mediocre, ignoring all signs of misfit.

Have you ever seen a person attempt to button jeans that are too small? They may roll on the bed, tugging and twisting, hold their breath in to flatten their stomach, ask another person to help, and make a scene. Such a display is entertaining. However, is this struggle what you want to apply to your life? Will you roll around on a bed or stop breathing until you accept your situation? This is not living! Trust me, I know from experience. My choice to place my career above all other things left me with many restless nights. Similar to putting on tight jeans, twisting, turning, and flipping became my nighttime experience.

THE GREAT FALL

Alas, I tortured myself because, in my mind, leaving work wasn't an option. Regardless of how tight the job became, new accounting rules, additional audits, shorter deadlines, and so on, I didn't budge. Instead, I was convinced that everything else, such as time with family and friends, personal hobbies, and other commitments, had to conform so my career could continue to "fit."

To obtain a "different" life, you must first choose to be uncomfortable. Indeed, the uncomfortable stages in life help to prune you so you may gain the qualities of becoming a person destined for purpose. For instance, losing a loved one is uncomfortable. Often, their death may cause you to question your faith—or life itself. But if you go through the grieving process, you will discover and develop strength, perseverance, and ultimately peace. You become stronger when you overcome the challenges of life. Being uncomfortable is consistent and severe, but it is necessary for growth and success.

COMFORTABILITY, A COMMON CHOICE

Some time ago, I met a business owner, Sarah. She told me she had an employee named John, who was not meeting her job requirements. Sarah frequently shared her concerns about John's poor performance with him. She explained he did not work efficiently, was not completing all the assigned tasks, and, sometimes, she had to question the accuracy of his work.

Nevertheless, although John was not delivering the results Sarah required, Sarah kept John as an employee. After over four years of unsatisfactory performance, Sarah started reprimanding John in writing to encourage productivity. After multiple reprimands, there was little difference in John's performance. Sarah couldn't put the finger on why her strategies hadn't worked.

Why did the written reprimands fail? The answer is simple. Both parties were comfortable. John was comfortable hearing the complaints regarding his performance (the previous verbal reprimands). At the same time, Sarah was comfortable with accepting his poor performance. As a result, the cycle continued. John

THE GREAT FALL

was not convinced that the written reprimands would change anything, not even cause a termination. And he was correct because, after twelve reprimands, John was still working for Sarah without any improvement

Now, if you should discuss this subject with either party, both individuals will have hours of information to share. For example, John would say that Sarah is impatient and frequently changed the required deadlines. At the same time, Sarah would complain that the requested items were always turned in late and often incorrect. Yet after various discussions between the two individuals, both parties returned to their old habits as neither individual would act differently.

Besides, John had been feeling underpaid from the beginning. Based on the average salaries for that position, John could receive an additional $20,000 a year for the level of work his boss required of him. However, he chose comfort by remaining with his current employer and receiving a meager salary.

COMFORTABILITY, A COMMON CHOICE

Here, John is sacrificing approximately $80,000 ($20,000 a year for four years) by keeping his current job. $80,000 is the amount John will forego to maintain his current position while avoiding all other opportunities. Economists would term the $80,000 as the opportunity cost, the money that a person loses by choosing one opportunity over the other. As John is still an employee for the same owner, this cost will continue to grow.

What is your opportunity cost of staying comfortable? Does your comfortability have a value or amount that you are leaving on the table for others to consume? Better yet, have you evaluated the maximum amount of money you are willing to leave behind to be comfortable? Do the math!

In this case, I can quantify the sacrifice someone is willing to make to be comfortable and associate comfortability to money. Maybe your opportunity cost doesn't relate to money. Could you be giving up wisdom, personal growth, mental stability, and other valuable gifts of life?

THE GREAT FALL

What if you are sacrificing something unmeasurable, for example, your health? What if a day at a stressful job result in a three-hour migraine? What if every day at a lackluster job brings you one day closer to a stroke?

Take the time to evaluate how much of your future and purpose you are willing to sacrifice. We often chose comfortability to avoid challenges. Most important, comfortability provides security, but this is a false sense of security, as the only thing you will be secure from is change and actively managing life.

Being uncomfortable is not desirable. Nevertheless, there are ways to overcome the temporary discomfort. I will discuss this further in the upcoming chapters.

CHAPTER 3

YOU VERSUS COMFORTABILITY

One thing you must have in mind is this: you must fight to be uncomfortable. Comfortability is easy to accept and revert to when faced with the challenges that accommodates uncomfortability. Comfortability is like a warm blanket during the winter. But often, comfortability provides a false sense of security. You must learn how to *overcome the uncomfortable feeling of being comfortable.*

Peter was comfortable in the old pants because he got used to them, not because they were comfortable to wear; they were tight. The new pants were uncomfortable at first because he was not used to them, and he wanted to return to what *he thought* was comfort, even though that was not true.

THE GREAT FALL

The new pants will eventually become comfortable for a while until you outgrow those. The cycle begins again between uncomfortable and comfortable.

Let us examine the six easy ways to conquer comfortability:

1. Evaluate Moments of Fear

Often, being uncomfortable means to agree to fail. Although most go to extraordinary steps to avoid failure, failure is the sincerest teacher. Failure tests your desires and challenges your intent to accomplish new goals. Failure is consistent and helps to develop tenacity. Everybody experiences the fear of failure. Hence, most people chose comfortability to avoid trying something new.

However, to operate beyond comfortability, first, acknowledge that fear will be a frequent visitor. To say you should not fear the "uncomfortable process" is unreasonable. Instead, observe when fear shows up so you can conquer it or take a position despite the fear.

YOU VERSUS COMFORTABILITY

Now, reflecting on the business owner, Sarah, and John, the employee, Sarah feared she would not find an employee with these three qualities she admired in John:

a. Honesty - John was always honest about the status of the assignments. Even when he didn't perform according to expectations.

b. Reliability - John came to work every day on time. Sarah could count on John being there.

c. Integrity - Sarah trusted John with the business's sensitive information and knew John wouldn't do anything to jeopardize the company purposely.

Sarah did not fire John because she was afraid. If she hired the wrong employee, she would have to repeat the search process for an extended period, as finding quality employees is always challenging.

Similarly, John feared going back into the market as a free agent as he was older than most candidates. He feared the challenges that are associated with finding a new job. He believed that his older age would be a disadvantage and would cause unemployment for an extended period.

Still, should the fear of training new employees or finding new employment overshadow being miserable eight hours a day, five days a week? Most people spend most of their lives at work. Is this how you want to remember your life, regretting every day?

One discussion between Sarah and John became so verbally hostile that John wanted to walk out. Working in a disgruntled environment is unhealthy for all parties. Can you imagine the effects such an environment is having on their mental and physical health? Again, John and Sarah are making choices to remain in an unpleasant environment daily due to fear.

Instead, you should use fear to inspire and motivate you. When faced with a decision, question whether you are hesitant due to robust discrepancies in the decision or fear. If fear is the primary reason, then press forward with change.

YOU VERSUS COMFORTABILITY

So, what did I fear? Changing jobs meant learning new job tasks, adjusting to new co-workers, and adapting to a new work environment. Although these are significant changes, my greatest fear was the lack of planning. Since college, I had learned to plan every part of my education and career to meet the long-term goals I created for myself.

Here I was, knowing that my time with my employer was ending, but I had nothing else. After five years of sacrifice, to walk away with nothing was unimaginable. Was it reasonable to believe that my emptiness inside would be filled with nothing? Common sense told me that zero and zero equals zero, and fear agreed. I had to contact a different source for encouragement.

2. Engage a Mentor

Many people have gone before you who have some level of experience and success in handling similar situations. You are not the first person to sit at a workstation you have outgrown. Many have experienced the desk or chair that only seems to welcome anxiety. When stepping out of your comfort zone, it is important to find someone, even several people, if needed, who have been where you are and have accomplished greatness after that.

A mentor can help you evaluate where you are in your career and where you aspire to be. They can expose you to different opportunities and even inspire you through the most fearful times. For instance, a mentor can help you evaluate whether a new job is truly an excellent opportunity or simply a job change. The difference between the two is whether the new job will develop you and your professional career in some aspect, particularly evolving you to reach your long-term goals. Certainly, a true job opportunity welcomes growth and development in some aspects. Also, a good mentor will explain that a salary increase does not necessarily equate to a job opportunity. A job opportunity should receive a full evaluation, including the job duties (learning opportunities),

YOU VERSUS COMFORTABILITY

growth potential within the company, company integrity, financial stability, responsibility, culture, and so on.

There was an accountant named Sam I mentored. He was working for a small company in which he performed accounting for various areas of the business, including account receivables, account payables, employee expenses, and purchasing. In summary, Sam's job exposed him to numerous areas of the company, allowing him to see how the company worked.

Over time, Sam sought other job opportunities, and he stumbled across a job position he felt was a better opportunity. As a mentor, I encouraged Sam to evaluate why the other position was a better opportunity. And Sam noted that the position was closer to home. We mapped the two locations from Sam's home and found that the distance was fairly the same. Sam then noted that the position provided additional responsibilities. Instead of managing the different areas of the business, the new position only involved account receivable transactions for over 25 customers. I challenged Sam to truly review the tasks of the two positions.

In the current position, Sam is involved in at least four areas (account receivables, account payables, employee expenses, and purchasing) of the business, whereas, in the new position, Sam is only involved in one area of the business (account receivables). After further discussion with Sam, he realized that the new position was not a true job opportunity that will develop Sam further in his career. Rather it was a demotion as it relates to his career path as his accounting exposure would decrease with the new position.

Mentors help to shed light where there is potential tunnel vision or bias as we frequently gravitate to items that appear to be shiny and new. As outsiders, mentors have nothing to gain or lose, and with their experience can interpret the real essence of a job position or career opportunity. Also, a mentor can interpret the commonly used industry jargon and breakdown actual expectations and tasks that may be advertised on the job listing.

When challenged with fear, you typically feel you are walking alone. If you are a believer, you always have a friend who not only walks with you but also carries you when you are weak.

Although a mentor cannot replace the impact God will have in challenging situations, a mentor can minimize feelings of loneliness you may experience. The advice of a mentor can carry you through your periods of fear. Even the thought of knowing you have a trusted friend can empower you to continue.

And, a mentor can help you prepare for the disasters to come. The attitude of a person aware of a potential challenge is different from a person caught completely by surprise. When informed, you can identify a challenge and strategize an effective plan. But a person without information loses focus and spends most of the time attempting to overcome the thought of

THE GREAT FALL

the challenge instead of tackling the challenge itself. A mentor can help you focus on the big picture and the process by which you can limit your time agonizing over issues.

A mentor can also expose you to a network of people and resources to assist you with your success. Many times, the step between you and your next level is the hand of someone contacting you to pull you up. A network of experienced professionals and resources, whether educational or financial, is invaluable. Having a network of experienced professionals is like having direct contact with legends. They can share the mistakes and best strategies and help you avoid common pitfalls. This is important as you will save time by not repeating the same failures.

Avoid the typical distractions of finding a mentor. For example, if entrepreneurship is your goal, for many of us, it will be challenging to locate the millionaire next door. There are many steps you must achieve to become a successful entrepreneur. Here is a secret: you do not need a millionaire as a mentor to become one

YOU VERSUS COMFORTABILITY

yourself. Simply, you should find a person who has achieved the level of success you would like to obtain.

As your journey progresses, engage new and additional mentors. Do not limit yourself to having only one mentor throughout your life. There is wisdom amongst the masses. Use the challenge for finding mentors as an opportunity to meet new people and ask questions. View this as gaining a network of experienced professionals in which you can develop healthy relationships.

So, where can you find potential mentors? Look for mentors at your local churches or community organizations. You may even find mentors at local businesses. Consider volunteering for causes that interest you to gain wisdom. Mentoring opportunities are available if you put in a little effort and affirm you are seeking one. There are even platforms today for hiring remote mentors for various goals. However, I prefer a physical relationship that a local mentor can provide.

THE GREAT FALL

3. Find Encouragement by Setting Goals

Uncountable emotions come with being uncomfortable. Yet they can be minimized with successful planning. First, set goals to carry out the vision. Create short-term and long-term goals throughout the process to ensure that you stay on track. Note that your short-term goals should guide you in accomplishing your long-term goals.

Short-term goals are daily, weekly, or monthly goals. The short-term goal's timing will be determined based on the time you can allocate. Of course, daily goals will allow you to stay more focused than the other timing options. While this may be true, a determination is purely heart-based. And, I do not advise having short-term goals defined beyond the monthly period as the extended time will allow for various distractions.

Write down the goals and allow them to be visible to you without searching for them. Make sure your goals are specific and have an expected completion date.

YOU VERSUS COMFORTABILITY

For example, an exercise goal would be to run a mile within five minutes by the end of next month. Specific goals will allow you to measure your efforts along the way and make impactful adjustments when deemed necessary.

Second, review and update the goals daily or as often as you can. A frequent review will keep you encouraged and inspired. The more you study the goals at hand, the higher the possibility of achieving the goals.

<u>4. Embrace Success</u>

Never miss the opportunity to celebrate success. Every time you achieve a goal, no matter how small, celebrate your achievement. Congratulations! You are one step closer to your success. Acknowledging the completion of milestones throughout the process allows you to see what being uncomfortable looks like in a different light.

Imagine you are a boxer. Every time you achieve a goal, you hit being uncomfortable with a one-two combo. Even if you endure twenty rounds, every combo weakens the opponent and encourages you to go back into the ring. You will eventually see that the "uncomfortable" giant can be defeated.

Then, write down all achievements and keep these where you can see them often. This documentation will be beneficial on the days or moments when you are convinced that comfortability was the winner and going forward will be impossible. When you read a list of accomplishments, your faith in yourself will revive, and you will find the strength to continue. Achieving purpose and success is difficult, but it is not impossible when you stay motivated.

5. Educate Yourself

You must seek knowledge and education. You will never know everything about a subject. When developing your career path, continuing your education is essential to stay relevant. The world is continuously changing. As such, it is imperative to continue to educate yourself through training, reading, classes, and experience. A person who stops learning ceases to exist.

Therefore, create a plan to stimulate yourself intellectually. Turn off the television and put down the electronics. Take time to read stimulating literature daily. Set a goal to read at least one book a month. With today's search capabilities, you can easily find a book on any topic. Ask your network of people (mentors, family, friends, and other professionals) for book recommendations that will assist you on your path. Most people will love to help! If you do not have a network of professionals, create one (as previously advised).

Furthermore, I understand that reading is not a hobby that many people enjoy. Nevertheless, knowledge will separate you from a colleague or competition. So, take the time out to ask questions and find answers.

Initially, I was not fond of reading. I was relying on people to educate me. But as I matured, I realized that

THE GREAT FALL

placing 100 percent of faith in people's ability to provide me with accurate information was lazy and irresponsible.

I met a small business owner named Clark, who hired a certified public accountant (CPA) to register the company and perform financial and tax reporting. I asked Clark a few questions regarding his business as the company's formation (i.e., incorporated, limited liability company, etc.), general liability insurance coverage, and tax filings. Do you know that Clark could not answer specific questions? He responded that his CPA did all the work, and it should be correct as he is paying the CPA a good salary.

Do you know that as a business owner, you must ensure your company is operating with integrity and within the local, state, and federal regulations? An owner saying, "His CPA handles everything," does not excuse the owner from any responsibilities or actions of the company. It would be a shame for Clark to realize that his company does not have proper general liability insurance after a company involved accident.

YOU VERSUS COMFORTABILITY

Consequently, the owner should be involved and at least understand tasks performed by hired professionals. Not that you must be an expert. In fact, that is why you hire professionals. However, do not solely rely on the professional's ability to do what is best for the company. Be involved by asking questions, reviewing information and documentation, comparing information from year to year to identify changes, and inquiring of other business owners in the same industry to assess industry standards. If all else fails, use the internet to research topics online. The point is, as an owner, once you hire someone, your role in that area does not stop.

In my case, I have developed a willingness to find answers and ensure that I understand the information related to my business. Sincerely, understanding is more important than locating the information. It may take me to read several books or articles to receive a full understanding. But once I obtain the knowledge, no one can take that asset from me.

<u>6. Exercise your ability to take on new tasks.</u>

THE GREAT FALL

One of my strengths, as it relates to the workplace, is my ability to be a chameleon. My typical role at a company is accounting related (i.e., credits, debits, balance sheet, income statement, and so on). However, over the years, I have participated in performing and managing tasks in other departments, including Human Resources, Information Technology, Payroll, Purchasing, and Operations. To be clear, I am not an expert in these subjects, but my previous experiences allow me to be comfortable in a conversation and willing to be involved in a related project. This comfortability was generated through my experiences, the willingness to take on opportunities in areas, which I had little to no knowledge or experience.

By taking on areas in which I was unfamiliar, I exposed myself to failure. So, what does that mean? Well, with taking on tasks in departments in which I was unaccustomed, I made various mistakes. Learning how to correct mistakes and accomplish goals, despite failures created many opportunities for me. In order to accomplish the goal, I had to tap into multiple resources, including educational literature and professionals in the crafts, to guide me through the process. I acknowledged and accepted that my success was not contingent on my knowledge, but my ability to locate answers and resolutions. Then, I developed a different mindset as it relates to errors, problems, or changes. While others may see them as a hindrance, I view them as an excellent opportunity to learn, develop, and network with other professionals.

How do these different experiences and skills automatically assist in my long-term security? Well, if I should need employment, I can apply for a diverse number of job opportunities as my experience expands beyond accounting. For instance, I can apply for a position in purchasing and receiving in the Operations department due to my purchasing and inventory experience. However, since I have not mastered those areas, I would apply for beginner positions. Of course, the salary I would receive would be

THE GREAT FALL

lower than an accounting position I qualify for. As noted, a job opportunity should not be purely salary based.

Consider this typical example. A beginner position may allow me to work from home as there is a growing number of work-from-home jobs that require entry-level employees. When evaluating the full benefits of accepting a position, I would consider the money saved from lunch, clothes, and commuting to and from work. Although the base salary for the position may be lower, the money saved may offset the lower base pay causing the job to be desirable. Additionally, the flexibility in the job position will allow me to focus on other opportunities (i.e., starting my own business); further increasing the job position's potential.

Another, beginner position may lead to a long-term managerial role. Asking the right questions during a job interview can reveal a company's true expectations and needs. Once the company's concerns are

YOU VERSUS COMFORTABILITY

discussed, I would use the information to create opportunities in the future. For instance, I interviewed for an Office Manager position. After assessing all the needs of the company, I was able to pitch possible grow opportunities to the owner; encouraging the creation of a new Controller position in which I would be considered for after a 90-day probationary period. Remember, during an interview, the employer is not only assessing if you are a good fit. Equally, you should be assessing whether the company and position align with your goals and expectations.

With my diverse experiences, I can start my own business since I have been involved in most aspects of running a business. If I should require additional information regarding a specific area in which I am not experienced, I know people and companies I can go to. For instance, there are a few recruiting firms I use regardless of my employer. I enjoy using the same contacts continuously, as they are accustomed to how

THE GREAT FALL

I work and respond. Most important, they provide results.

CHAPTER 4

DELAYS DUE TO CONTINGENCIES

Sometimes, desires are nourished by delays. With this in mind, I decided to assist my son with the challenge ahead. My first task was to convince Peter to keep his new pants on. Peter did not feel secure in the looser-fitting pants because the feeling was new and different. I was determined to convince Peter to make the right choice.

In pure mother-mode, I asked Peter to model the pants for me, and provided over-the-top reactions, "Oooooo! Baby, those pants look good on you! You look so handsome in that outfit! I bet you can run fast in those pants; show me!"

THE GREAT FALL

Therefore, after much convincing, Peter was willing to step outside of his comfort zone, but this was subject only to a specific request. He required an object that would secure the pants in place: a belt.

After all the efforts I made, there were still more requests. Does this sound familiar in any way? Have you received numerous signs that point towards a new job? However, your acceptance of a new direction is solely contingent on the fulfillment of further requests and requirements. For instance, you may say, "I will leave this stressful job once I find my dream job."

Do you try to use the same method to meet your desired goal, perhaps trying to bargain with God? For example, "God, I will be obedient if you deliver me from this illness." "God, I will serve you, if only you'll help me navigate through this horrendous storm."

Although this thought-process is not inappropriate as there is a natural tendency to think this way, it will delay progress towards your ultimate goals as God

DELAYS DUE TO CONTINGENCIES

will only assist as He will expect you to play a part. Even when you receive the things you ask for, in many cases, you may make no efforts to accept the change truly. You will use the contingencies primarily to justify the lack of progress towards getting something better.

The truth is, you are the only one who possesses the intensity for you to succeed. Unlike a mother who is trying to help her son, there are only a few individuals that will have the same overwhelming desire to assist you. All the same, if you're lucky, you may have a loving parent who is willing to go the extra mile. But should a parent risk their retirement goals, pension, or savings to assist you with your success?

One thing I can assure you of is, you can make requests for you to move beyond comfort. However, awaiting assistance will only leave you with dreams unfulfilled. Congratulations, you are a dreamer!

There are many dreamers in the world, but very few achievers. According to the book, *A Century of*

THE GREAT FALL

Wealth in America by Edward N. Wolff, one of the world's great experts on the economics of wealth in America, as of 2016, twenty percent of households own ninety percent of the wealth. The twenty percent have an average net worth of $3 million. You can see these individuals are the achievers. The remaining eighty percent share only ten percent of the wealth. You can categorize these people as the dreamers. This would seem to indicate that it is acceptable to be a dreamer. According to Wolff, twenty percent of the eighty percent have an average net worth of $273,600. That is impressive compared to other developing countries. Yet, are you destined to be more and have more?

Think about this. Many individuals apply this contingency theory when working towards their purpose or leaving an unfulfilling work position. One may say, "I will leave my current job when I find another." This is not an incorrect approach, but I challenge you to think differently. You can find other ways to achieve

DELAYS DUE TO CONTINGENCIES

greatness without committing one hundred percent to your current job.

For instance, it is recommended to leave a current job only if you have a new job in place. However, I challenge you to be creative; this is a unique step in the right direction. Imagine it will take approximately six months to two years to build a new business or to become an entrepreneur. Consider leaving the current position once you have saved enough money to pay at least two years' worth of personal expenses. The two-year timeframe will help sustain your lifestyle while the business is growing to reach its full potential.

Additionally, you can work on the new business while working in your current position. There are twenty-four hours in a day, approximately thirty-three percent or 8 hours of the day is used for resting. That leaves sixty-seven percent or 16 hours for productivity. If you work during the weekdays for 8 hours, then you have 8 hours per day on weekdays and 16 hours per day on weekends for a total of 72 hours per week to commit to your new business. Of course, you would like to participate in other activities that life offers. However, my point is to show you the possible time you can allocate towards your goals.

Simply put, a well-structured and highly organized day will allow you to accomplish your entrepreneurial goals. Mind you, do not let your future to be contingent on more time. Because as you age, time and availability are not increasing. Therefore, if your success is contingent on more time, then you will never arrive.

Perhaps, you can be creative and make more availability. Consider working part-time or work from home (previously discussed) jobs with flexible hours to subsidize for the wages missed through leaving the current job. Note that the part-time job will not have to replace 100% of your income, but enough money is needed to maintain your personal needs and not wants.

DELAYS DUE TO CONTINGENCIES

Maybe it is time to re-evaluate how you spend your money. To be successful, you must learn to make sacrifices. Often, you'll have to give priority to essential things: choose to give up cable television, new clothes and shoes, and updated cell phones today to succeed in the future.

In my case, I ventured out into real estate investing. To encourage change, I knew I needed to have a secondary source of income to help support my family. After months of research, real estate seminars, and classes, I invested in my first rental property. The rental income equated to only seven percent of my monthly income. However, it was a step toward having another source of income- passive income.

Therefore, never allow excuses to convince you that you cannot accomplish something different. Contingencies are simply convincing excuses to stay where you are, avoiding all growth potential.

THE GREAT FALL

Peter agreed to wear the new pants using the contingency theory, "I will wear the new pants if I am provided with a belt to hold the pants up." Between you and me, the belt added no additional stability, as the pants were not that loose. Peter just needed to feel secure.

Security is a highly desirable feeling. Numerous decisions are made based on the level of security it provides. However, security should be the long-term and not the short-term goal as you advance your career. As previously noted, during the early stages of your career, you should pursue opportunities that provide growth through training, personal, and professional development instead of security.

Security allows you to play it safe. A significant distinction between a dreamer and an achiever is the ability to take on risk. During the earlier moments of your career, time is favorable, as you will be allowed to fail and recover as often as needed. In essence, you should consider reprioritizing the level of importance

DELAYS DUE TO CONTINGENCIES

to which security plays in decision making. If opportunities are used appropriately, the skills, knowledge, and expertise you acquire will automatically invest in your long-term security.

As Peter requested security, I rushed to locate a belt. I have succeeded in convincing my son to make the right choice. The least I could do was to find a belt to assist him along the way.

CHAPTER 5

THE RESULTS FROM RUSHING

Often, we get obsessed with speed. And so, we move swiftly to get things done more efficiently. Despite our desperate effort to keep up, we realize that we might be hurting more than helping.

For me, my accident started as I ran down the stairs with a belt in hand to assist my son with his current insecurities. After my son put on the clothes I laid out on his bed; he came downstairs to complain about the pants he had on. I ran up the stairs to his bedroom to find a belt. Once I found the belt, I was excited to bring it to Peter. My eagerness led me to run down the stairs. The excitement I had was necessary and vital to keep the drive for purpose. The misstep was the running and rushing of deliverables.

How often in life have we run from insecurity to rush to purpose? For instance, financial insecurity may encourage frequent job-hopping because a job change (in certain industries) equates to an increase in pay.

For this reason, to obtain "social" security, we may date numerous individuals or have various strict rules or limitations around dating (relationships must be defined within three months). It is almost as if there is never enough time to develop security and live a purposed-filled life.

However, before choosing to be uncomfortable, we seemed to have plenty of time to remain stuck in comfortable situations. Simultaneously, we were developing various excuses for remaining the same and waiting for many years before stepping out on faith.

So, why do we place these pressures on time as it relates to success and purpose? Are we running from

THE RESULTS FROM RUSHING

insecurity, or are we rushing towards a purpose? Either way, if you allowed yourself to be stuck for five years, the least you can do is allow five years to develop security and purpose. Why are we so impatient when headed in the right direction? I know we get anxious when we finally figure out things in life. However, we cannot allow anxiety to corrupt our future.

Come to think of it, what if I told you that rushing and anxiety are mental tricks resulting from the decision to be uncomfortable, different, and intentionally great? The purpose of the trick is to convince you that the change you chose to make was not the right decision. Unconsciously, you may place strict deadlines on the plan to prove the new path's incompetency, but it is all a mental game.

The Bible passage found in Ephesians 6:12[1] discusses spiritual warfare:

> "For we wrestle not against flesh and blood, but principalities, against powers, against the rulers of

the darkness of this world, against spiritual wickedness in high places."

Now, what if I told you a secret? The scripture speaks of war. This war is against the spiritual forces of evil and not against flesh and blood. What if I told you that the first battle is within yourself-- your mentality? Whereby you are subjected to unrelenting attacks in your thoughts, which comes in the form of anxiety, depression, fear, doubt, worry, and other maladies of these kinds.

The good news is, you will become powerful when you have control over your thought life, (imaginations) and can cleanse your mind of the things that easily distract you or tell you how you do not measure up.

As we rush to find security and purpose, have we ever considered what is left behind in the "rush"? Probably, before you left that job, your boss was considering you for a promotion. However, you left the company before the promotion could be communicated.

THE RESULTS FROM RUSHING

Maybe your boyfriend had the engagement ring selected but was waiting on a holiday bonus to purchase the ring. The fact is, in the rushing process, we lose the purity of evolution.

Have you seen a disabled butterfly? Probably not, because they do not control the process. Development from caterpillar to butterfly perfection is slow and steady. Thus, any pressure to shorten the developmental process from caterpillar to butterfly may weaken the insect and stop the transformation from taking place. Ultimately the butterfly will not emerge. Depending on the timing in which the chrysalis is agitated, soupy liquid may ooze out, confirming no further development.

Let us investigate the caterpillar transformation process. The transformation begins with a hungry caterpillar who travels from place-to-place eating leaves to grow long and plump. Once the caterpillar is full, it hangs upside down from a twig and spins into a chrysalis or cocoon. While in the cocoon, the caterpillar digests itself, going through an intense internal

THE GREAT FALL

metamorphosis. At the end of the process, the insect is transformed and emerges as a butterfly.

Like the caterpillar, it is not until you are hungry for more essential things that you are ready for a real transformation. You may go from place-to-place or multiple people and jobs attempting to fill the emptiness inside, not realizing that the answer is within yourself all the time. If only you take the time needed to properly develop yourself mentally, professionally, economically, and physically, you will become a beautiful adult who willfully displays the colorful experiences that transformed you into the purposed-filled person God has created you to become.

Like the caterpillar, everything you need to transform into a beautiful butterfly was provided when you were born. It is not a coincidence you look the way you do, have the family you have, or have the talents and interests you have. These qualities are all necessary for the transformation. The issues in the developmental process stem from the way you internalize

THE RESULTS FROM RUSHING

who you are designed to be. When you compare yourself to your neighbors and see yourself based on other people's views, you damage your mentality and weaken your transformation. Once you learn to appreciate who you are, in no time, you will learn to fly.

Naturally, if you do not wait for the allotted time, your dreams will have no choice but to either develop with imperfections or die due to rushing.

Your challenge is to slowly build security, ensuring a solid foundation, and assurance about your decisions. Take the appropriate time to avoid regrettable moments.

THE STUMBLE

CHAPTER 6

FOCUS, A NECESSITY

I was running down the stairs holding a belt in my right hand, and I held the railing with my left. I found myself more excited about the delivery of security than running down the stairs. I stumbled at step number eleven.

Why did I stumble? The answer is simple: I lost focus.

My lack of focus reminded me of a famous story in the Bible involving Jesus and His disciple, Peter. Peter was on a boat with other disciples when Jesus appeared to them, walking on water towards the boat. Peter asked Jesus if he should come out onto the water with Him. Jesus answered, telling Peter to come.

THE GREAT FALL

After taking a few steps on the surface of the water, Peter became afraid and began to sink.

Peter sank because he removed his focus from Jesus to the wind surrounding him. When he fixed his gaze on Jesus, he walked on water. But, his change of focus from Jesus to the storm surrounding him led to the havoc. Like Peter, I fell because I removed my concentration from navigating steps to my excitement. I had found a belt for my son!

Peter miraculously took a few steps on the water, but how great could the miracle have been if Peter had stayed focused on Jesus?

You see, focus is necessary for destiny. It is necessary to grow your vision and purpose. You gain success quickly when you remain focused throughout the process. To see someone fail in an endeavor, find something the person will lose focus on.

Have you ever evaluated the power of addictions? It's not the item that the person is addicted to that has the power. If that were the case, there would not be

FOCUS, A NECESSITY

multiple addictions. For instance, there is drug addiction, sex addiction, alcohol addiction, gaming addiction, food addiction, and many others. If the power was in the substance or activity alone, then the list would be minimal and include only particular items. Some of these items have strong influential characteristics to entice addiction. But, the power of addiction is that the thing—whatever it may be—distracts the person from other aspects of life, narrowing their focus to only the desire of their addiction. In reality, anything can be an addiction, ranging from the physical to the emotional, such as sugar or self-pity.

Do you have an addiction that is holding you back from your purpose? By chance, are you addicted to being comfortable? What about an addiction to complaining? Are you addicted to giving up?

Maybe your issue is not lack of focus, but the ever-revolving door of temporary distractions. How often in life do you set goals and become lured in other directions by unrelated items? You become so easily distracted by things in life: financial and family dysfunction, illness, divorce—even small successes. Understand that one turn of the eye can dissolve or blur the vision of the ultimate path you so desire.

When walking towards purpose, it is challenging to focus on the tasks at hand. Because you will notice opportunities coming from all directions, such as, a new job, an increase in salary, new relationships. You may also notice hardships such as losing friendships, an overwhelming number of challenges, an unsupportive spouse, and so on. All these are merely stumbling blocks to keep you from pursuing your purpose.

However, one way to know you are operating in purpose is to evaluate the number of problems you have encountered within a period. Also, evaluate how many people you have in your support group. If the problems are many and the friends are few, then you are headed in the right direction.

So, how do you stay on task?

FOCUS, A NECESSITY

1) Write daily tasks that will assist you with the vision. Consistency is vital to achieving any goal. Ceaseless drops of water will soon make a mighty ocean. So, define and display the tasks in a highly visible place such as on your smartphone screensaver or refrigerator. The daily tasks should complement the short-term and long-term goals noted in the previous chapters.

2) Revisit incomplete tasks from the previous day. Reprioritize the incomplete tasks as priority number one and complete them as soon as possible.

3) Build an attitude of resilience. Create and maintain an attitude of perseverance to endure the numerous attacks. Ensure you meditate daily, either first thing in the morning or later at night. Meditation helps to rebalance you mentally so you can be prepared for what may come ahead. Meditation, coupled with daily goal reviews, will keep you focused on the tasks at hand.

4) Initiate an accountability system. Throughout the process of fulfilling purpose, you will find yourself by yourself. So, intentionally create a support system. Find an individual in pursuit of something great, just like you. Allow them to ask you the questions that cause you to be the most insecure and ensure you are honest with the answers. Questions such as:

» What have you accomplished in the past weeks that allowed you to get closer to achieving your goals?

» What have you allowed to distract you from the task ahead of you? What are your plans to prevent such distractions in the future?

» What excuse are you using this week that are continuously holding you back?

5) Make your efforts intentional. Often, you may be clouded with the thought of how long it will take to obtain your desired result. You can become so overwhelmed by the vision that the fulfillment

FOCUS, A NECESSITY

may appear untouchable. However, daily application and celebration of small achievements will encourage you to continue.

CHAPTER 7

CONSISTENT UNTIL THE END

There are fourteen steps on my staircase. When I stumbled, I stumbled on the eleventh step. So, what is the significance of stumbling at step number eleven? That number is towards the end of accomplishing the goal or vision at hand. It is the time when, typically, you will find yourself most distracted and wanting to give up. It is the time that you need to gather all the faith, hope, and determination to push on to accomplish the tasks at hand.

Giving up the race when you are only a few feet away from the finish line is a common mistake most people make. You may know someone who dropped out of college during their junior or senior year.

THE GREAT FALL

Most people will say that's insane: "How can someone give up when they are so close?" Usually, individuals are most vulnerable when they are a few steps to the finish line.

Just think, when you first start a race, you have so much energy and emotion. You may be nervous, anxious, and all-around pumped for the race to begin. The adrenaline remains with you until about the half-way point. However, when you have completed seventy-five percent of the race, you are exhausted and fatigued. You start considering giving up. It is then the race becomes less about your physical ability and more about your mental state.

This is when many of us lose the race due to mental malnutrition. You place most of your training efforts in building the outward appearance or physical abilities. However, you fail in conditioning yourself spiritually and mentally.

One of the oldest stories told is of the tortoise and the hare. The most common moral of the story is

CONSISTENT UNTIL THE END

that the tortoise won because he was slow and steady. Regardless of the version of this story, you may have heard. The hare was focused on everything but the race. The hare wanted to be fast, then he wanted to eat a snack, and then he wanted to take a nap, and so on, while the tortoise was focused, "slow and steady" wins the race.

The tortoise was mentally prepared and able to remain focused on the task. On the other hand, the hare was scattered-brained and prideful. Although the hare appeared to be capable physically, the tortoise was mentally prepared and ultimately won the race. The tortoise was consistent and focused.

Like the hare, when you hit the three-fourths-done marker of the race, you are ready to take a nap. You think the nap will rejuvenate you and encourage you to finish the race. However, you would be wiser to mimic the tortoise and not rest until the race is over. A break, which is the typical reaction at this time, will seem like the answer. Instead, it is a significant distraction. It is easy to believe you will take a short

THE GREAT FALL

break to resume later. What you may not realize is once you take the break, the "right time to resume" may never come.

THE FALL

CHAPTER 8

GOING DOWN

As I stumbled downstairs eleven through fourteen, attempting to regain my balance along the way, I told myself just to fall. So, I released my hold on the belt and the railing, bent backward, and fell. While lying at the bottom of the stairs, I learned three valuable lessons:

1) Every step is necessary.

2) Sometimes it is just easier to fall.

3) You must have a confident attitude while gaining altitude.

Now, let me further explain these lessons to you.

Lesson 1: Take Life Step-By-Step

THE GREAT FALL

No doubt, life is challenging. I am sure if someone invented shortcuts to life, that person would be a multi-billionaire. Although you probably wish you could take the less challenging route in life, skip some steps, and just navigate to others. But I want you to know that each step is necessary. Because there are lessons, you must learn and be exposed to, especially those lessons where you endure unlikely circumstances.

Many parents advise their children to attend college to obtain a higher education. The hope is that the college student will be challenged to solve problems and learn foundations and theories. However, it is not until the student becomes an employee at their first job that the student learns accurate application. Although the levels of education are essential and provide the needed foundation, life experiences remain the true teachers. Education is great and helps a person to grow, but life experiences increase the value of an individual.

As previously noted, I stumbled, starting at step number eleven. However, after the fall, I was positioned at

GOING DOWN

step number nine. Like my fall, avoiding steps may cause repeating previously accomplished steps. You end up moving in circles because each step is crucial for self-development. One step may expose your strengths while another may build your humility. Each step has its place and purpose. Therefore, the more steps missed, the longer and harder the fall.

As it relates to your purpose and timing, a missed step may equal a three-month delay. So, three steps missed will cause a nine-month delay. Now, you will learn more through the delayed process. However, some lessons you endure may result from taking shortcuts. A "true shortcut" is going through the plan without adding unnecessary delays. Added delays will build tenacity and endurance, but I assume you would prefer to avoid any additional efforts or sacrifices.

When you find yourself being anxious, review the vision and the list of goals. This review will remind you to follow the process while walking down every step.

However, while following the plan, don't forget to enjoy every moment, both challenging and routine.

Lesson 2: Sometimes It is Easier to Fall

It is human nature to fix problems or put on a facade as though an issue doesn't exist. For instance, some of us go to work smiling on the outside while feeling miserable on the inside. Some pretend to be "fine" to make it through the workday. Others may continue to invest in items like clothing, cars, and toys, purchasing status. They do this while being thousands of dollars in debt or barely able to make ends meet, living at the mercy of each paycheck. To this person, living the "good life" in appearance overshadows the hurt and pain that hunger and homelessness brings.

Although Halloween is a day where you are encouraged to wear costumes, the truth is, many of us wear costumes daily and have attached our name to it permanently. We convince ourselves to believe that the mask we are wearing provides the "balance" (mostly in appearance) that our life needs.

GOING DOWN

Those who are financially stressed, mask their reality in loans. Loans like payday loans are used to bridge finances from one paycheck to the other, ultimately hiding the real issue and problem in their financial life.

Why is this so important? When we misstep, we are the most vulnerable. When we fall, our exposed selves are front and center; all masks are off and are down beside us. It is difficult to save yourself from falling while holding a mask. Similar to me holding the belt in my hand. But, when falling, everything is released to save the most important thing, yourself.

Have you ever seen someone trip in public? They do everything in their power to appear that the trip was on purpose or otherwise attempt to cover up their misstep. It is entertaining to see the lengths people will go to avoid others seeing them fall—to avoid others seeing their exposed selves.

THE GREAT FALL

Well, the New Year's Day fall taught me that such trickery is not always necessary. Instead of pretending that I did not make a mistake, it was easier to acknowledge the mistake, learn from the mistake, and move forward.

This principle can be helpful and applied to various aspects of life. If you make a terrible financial decision, evaluate why the decision was not the appropriate decision, acknowledge the root cause of the wrong decision, attempt to reverse the mistake, and remember the effects of the decision to avoid reoccurrence.

You may also use the concept with people in relationships. People can minimize arguments if they accept the fall instead of striving for perfection. Know when to swallow pride and fall, as I did. With a smile on my face, I let go, leaned back, and fell.

Did I have other options? Sure, I did. I could have continued to hold the railing until I gained my balance. But, at what cost? I may dismantle the railing when applying my weight and pressure. Fracture my ankle while attempting to recover from the different dispositions the misstep caused? Something much worse?

The thought of falling was scary and unknown. However, I chose the option I feared. In return, I received a gift; I was able to control how I fell. The fall was the slowest yet, the softest route to the floor.

You can apply the same concept to life. Failure will occur, and depression will come knocking; however, you can control how to accept or respond to either. You will realize that the situation or failure was not as bad as it seemed once you accepted it with an open mind.

I advise you to fall. Fall with intent. Fall with purpose. Fall with the right perception.

Lesson 3: Attitude While Gaining Altitude

Have you ever noticed that bad days appear to be longer than good days? It almost feels like bad days include 30 hours instead of 24, and out of all those

THE GREAT FALL

hours, you only slept for four. A good day, on the other end, zooms by as if there were only 18 hours, and you slept for 10.

This time illusion is because you dread hard times, days, minutes, and seconds. When faced with challenging events or falling into difficult situations, you are so uncomfortable that it seems as if time has slowed down to allow life to extend the cruelty. As a result, you get in such a hurry to put the uncomfortable event in your past.

Mentally, you want to speed up time to get to the end: the point in which you can assess the injuries, dust yourself off, and get back up. While falling, you are disgruntled, ashamed, and unappreciative that life has given you such a present. You treat life's challenges or falls as the unwanted Christmas gift you would love to return, re-gift, or throw in the closet, hoping never to see again. However, if you alter your attitude while going through difficulties, you can learn so much and be more conscious of the opportunities surrounding the fall.

GOING DOWN

When I fell, I gained control of the situation, which was the blessing, as any attempt to correct the misstep would have placed me in an uncontrollable situation. I fell without injury and hit the ground with a smile on my face. Most importantly, the fall gave me a revelation worth sharing with the world.

So, when you fall with the right perception, you open your mind to accept more than a specific situation. Learn how to truly live and appreciate the advances and the falls life offers.

You learn to eliminate the mindset of having only joy when times are good. This is necessary because, challenging times help you to discover how strong, knowledgeable, and encouraging you are to others. You are challenged to live daily as examples of Jesus Christ and His love that others may be convinced to follow Him.

However, how can you have a testimony without a test? How do you assess what you have learned without being challenged? How do you extend grace to

THE GREAT FALL

others without being hurt? All these opportunities are available to experience: the peace that surpasses all understanding, the irrevocable joy, likewise an unconditional love.

You may disagree with me and feel when life is going well; you are jovial, loving, and peaceful. And I do not disagree. However, it is easy to love and be happy when times are good. Happiness takes little effort when you are having a good day. However, those good-day feelings are merely surface-deep.

Let me prove it to you. Let someone unexpectedly tell you "no" or provide a negative comment about something you are passionate about. At least for a moment, a negative feeling or self-pity may follow. That a mere incident can change your feelings is proof that the good day feelings are only surface-deep. But if you have peace that surpasses all understanding, a "no" or negative response may be viewed as a sign of encouragement to keep going.

GOING DOWN

As you are traveling towards greatness, your attitude must be consistent through the good and the difficult times. The excitement and enthusiasm you feel when everything is perfectly aligned, and following the plan should be the same when you are continually being rejected. You cannot maintain surface feeling as they are too temporary for the journey. You must gain and maintain strength from an Eternal source. This, by far, is not a simple task.

THE AUDIENCE

CHAPTER 9

THERE IS ALWAYS SOMEONE WATCHING

Whenever you face a challenging time in life, doesn't it seem as if multiple people have front-row seats to watch your demise? Well, my entire family witnessed me gracefully fall down numerous steps; each member having different viewpoints. Where my audience stood mattered because it determined how well they saw what transpired.

After I landed on my back, I looked at my family members. Partially, because once you are on the floor, the natural reaction is to look up, but mostly to see if anyone would come rushing to my aid. While observing my family members, the one thing that stood out the most was their individual reaction to the incident.

THE GREAT FALL

Now, the reactions to the fall do not reflect the attitude of my family members. But a specific portion of each person's reaction helped me to identify future audience members (people who are typically around to witness a fall) and how their roles may change as you strive for professional success.

The audience members can vary. In my case, they were family members, but the mix can include strangers, family, and friends. It is imperative that you identify the individual audience members in your life as you get closer to the desired career path to anticipate how to deal with them under the circumstances.

CHAPTER 10

AUDIENCE MEMBER 1:

THE NON-REACTOR

My husband is downstairs watching a movie. Suddenly, he hears a loud thumping caused by my fall. From the floor, I see my husband raise his reclining chair, turn around to face me, asking, "Are you okay?" I nod yes, and he returns to watching the movie. At that moment, I recognize the first audience member: The Non-Reactor.

The Non-Reactor witnesses something, checks to see if they are needed, and if not, carry on their way. The Non-Reactor will spare a small portion of time to be distracted but wants to hurry back to their tasks.

THE GREAT FALL

The Non-Reactor understands that life happens and chooses not to overreact to another person's situation, especially if the damages are minimal. This is not to indicate that such an individual lacks compassion. However, they believe that going out of their way to assist others takes away from their success and limits the achievement of goals.

Although you and this audience member may be friends, the Non-Reactor may see you as competition. Of course, the Non-Reactor will not tell you directly that they view you as a competitor. However, you should be able to tell from their actions. For example, you may be at a point in your journey where you need a resource, such as an editor for a book. The Non-Reactor may know someone, but will not volunteer the information. He feels that you should put in the effort yourself and develop your own resources.

A Non-Reactor can also be identified in conversation. Have you ever known someone who, any time you mention something new or relay a situation, always seems to have had the same experience? Not only is

THE NON-REACTOR

it the same experience, somehow, but their experience is also more exciting or notable than yours every time. Say you share a story of being at a restaurant and receiving a complimentary drink. The Non-Reactor will tell you they went to the same restaurant on the same week and not only received a complimentary drink, but their entire meal was free. The Non-Reactor has no issue with exaggerating the matter if it allows him to appear slightly superior to the listener.

Ironically, you will seek a relationship with this audience member as they will have many things that will help you succeed. They may be in a similar position as you on their journey. However, you will find their time and attention to be a challenge within itself.

Be warned. This audience will not disclose their lack of interest in you achieving your purpose. However, their actions will reveal their identity. You may find yourself in a circle of their misrepresentations. For example, they may offer to assist you, but they never follow through with help. Since you are not only looking for assistance but approval, you may delay your progress, waiting on the Non-Reactor's efforts, which rarely, if ever, appear.

Occasionally, the Non-Reactor may eventually come to your rescue. However, this will be only after you have picked yourself up. Should you accept their assistance, do not get your hopes up, as the Non-Reactor's involvement will be sporadic and limited. Remain cautious so as not to fall into their unsuccessful circle of misrepresentation.

It is not unusual that my husband was the Non-Reactor during the accident. One of the least discussed topics between a husband and wife is how to balance career goals and aspirations within the family.

When a man and a woman are joined in matrimony, each individual enters the union with their idea of the future, including career goals, family size, and holiday traditions. Therefore, during the dating process, each individual shares their ideas of the future. But it

THE NON-REACTOR

is not until after the union, that the couple is challenged with balancing each person's career goals. You see, there are two individuals, each having a vision for the family. After matrimony, the expectation is to merge the two visions as one. The conflict is deciding which career path takes precedent and the timing in which transition occurs.

Without proper and frequent discussions and planning, spouses can become Non-Reactors. Each of them solely focusing on their career, attempting to prove their value toward the family economics to validate the continuance of their professional goals. The longer the couple delays the discussion, the more aggressive the competition. A competition which originated from career goals ignites competition in parenting, household chores, and financial responsibilities. Thus, the couple resents each other, and division occurs in the marriage. As the family grows and children are involved, additional pressures may be placed on the couple. Due to the family dynamics, inevitably, one spouse will be forced to halt their career aspirations to allow flexibility to ensure family commitments are met.

In contrast, the other spouse solely embodies the ideologies of the Non-Reactor, self-involved, and available briefly to ensure everything is running smoothly. By default, timely career advancement becomes an implied expectation for the Non-Reactor spouse to support the family better. Any deviations will cause the other spouse to explode as their choice to sacrifice their career would not appear to be justified.

CHAPTER 11

AUDIENCE MEMBER 2:

THE PROMOTER

The Promoter can sometimes be mislabeled as a close friend. The Promotor is there encouraging you, dancing with you, and always around to have fun. The Promotor will also be incredibly supportive. However, during the fall, the Promotor will appear with an "air blaster" behind your back. To elaborate further, they will not intentionally cause you harm. However, they are pleased with seeing you fall. The Promoter will find delight while you fall down the stairs.

The Promoter has goals. They run and fall just as you do. The difference is that they find joy in someone else's pain. Ironically, this gives them hope. The hope

THE GREAT FALL

is not derived from the thought that progress requires falls, and we all experience them, rather, if they are having trouble accomplishing their goals, they are glad to see you are, too. I am sure you have heard the phrase "misery loves company." Well, the Promotor embraces and embodies that statement completely.

Promoters are fun to be with and appear to be part of your reliable support system. Yet, when you experience a fall, a positive attitude, humility, and a sense of humor are necessary to avoid emotional exposure generated from the Promoter, since the Promoter will have no problem sharing your falls, flaws, and faults with others. If they could have recorded the fall, the video would have been posted on all their social media accounts, and you would be the star of their new viral meme.

During a fall, the Promoter always seems to have the best view. In my case, the Promoter was positioned at the top of the stairs looking down on every highlight of the fall. The Promotor's position during the fall is essential. In 1970, a psychologist named Richard

THE PROMOTER

Gregory coined the "Top-Down Processing Theory," which notes top-down perception is influenced by existing knowledge, beliefs, and expectations, meaning that a person uses their previous understanding and knowledge to deduce an outcome.

So, when I stumbled on stair number eleven, the Promoter expected for me to fall. Although the fall was not immediate as I stumbled on three additional stairs before electing to fall, the Promotor provided no support, intent on rescuing, or any other options to influence a different outcome. There was no flinch or unconscious movement to aid. As you develop your career, keep your paths and visions hidden from the Promoter. The Promoter will use your past failures and other people's inabilities to keep you from progress. The Promoter will ensure that they point out your shortcomings and lack of achievements. They will tout your many falls, misdirecting your focus to your failures without ever acknowledging any success. Moreover, the Promoter will use your history to constrict your abilities and limit your mindset.

THE GREAT FALL

Constant interaction with the Promoter will be emotionally draining.

After the fall, the Promotor will show compassion and ask if you are okay. However, the emotional and physical investment in your situation will be temporary. The Promotor will be so focused on the fall, that they will have no room to assist you with standing up. They will emphasize what they knew and attempt to communicate regarding the situation.

CHAPTER 12

AUDIENCE MEMBER 3:

THE EXCUSER

The Excuser will deflect the purpose of the fall as a part of the process—or the result of specific actions such as losing focus—to ultimately being the fault of others. For instance, they will say the fall came not from rushing or losing focus, but rather because "the strength of the gusty wind overwhelmed you and pushed you to the ground!" Of course, that is an exaggeration. A more straightforward reaction is to say: "If Peter did not request the belt, then there would not have been a fall." Simply put, The Excuser provides an excuse for everything and never wants to assume responsibility or admit that falling is part of the learning process.

THE GREAT FALL

The Excuser can be tricky because they can mask as a third party (External Excuser) or, perhaps, you are The Excuser yourself (Internal Excuser). A third-party Excuser will be easier to identify and to disassociate from once known. However, The Internal Excuser is challenging to spot and hard to admit to. The Excuser, whether a third-party or internal, can be dangerous. Believing the Excuser can lead to self-pity and, more seriously, depression.

The External Excuser

The Excuser is probably the most frequent audience member I encounter in the workplace. During my career, I have supervised numerous individuals. Many of the new hires had one thing in common; they were Excusers. When you ask an Excuser questions regarding the progress of assigned tasks, a typical response includes reasons the tasks are not complete instead of where they are in the process.

Let us be clear. The Excuser will not answer the question asked. However, as though justifying himself, the reasons why the task is incomplete will overshadow failing to meet desired expectations. When the Excuser asks for performance feedback, I simply reply, "I am waiting on you to let go of your excuses." This usually begins a productive conversation between the Excuser and I regarding expectations, duties, timing, and responsibilities. As excuses are merely time fillers, they add no value to any conversation or productivity.

The Internal Excuser

Developing an Internal Excuser is a defense mechanism created by the person to substantiate the lack of production or progression in any area of life. This mask allows the person to excuse themselves from all circumstances. In fact, becoming an Excuser is a learned behavior that develops over time to minimize disappointment from oneself or others. A person who grew up experiencing disappointments from any or many pertinent individuals—a mother, father, sibling, teacher, spouse—may develop an Internal Excuser. We derive these disappointments from people

THE GREAT FALL

close to us who never kept their promises, or from various individuals you wish to count on. Developing the Excuser is typically the result of being disappointed on so many occasions. This starts from sheer self-preservation.

To say that separating yourself from The Internal Excuser is as easy as recognizing the issue and changing is impractical. The critical notation is that the Excuser is seen as a protector and the hinderer. When the Excuser is internal, the path to purpose will be strenuous. You must first overcome double-mindedness (desiring greatness and moving towards it versus dealing with all the obstacles that others are "intentionally" placing in your path). The hope of success must overshadow the developed pessimistic attitude and multiplicity of excuses.

CHAPTER 13

AUDIENCE MEMBER 4:

YOU

When falling, you will notice that the closer you get to the ground, the bigger the audience and the feeling of loneliness. It is incredible how numerous people can surround you, and you still find *yourself* by *yourself*. Do not be alarmed. This is part of the process. Now, there are key characteristics you must develop on your way to success. And managing loneliness is one of them. Do not separate yourself to where you miss the essential part of the performance. However, keep some goals a secret to keep your dreams alive. There is nothing like entertaining negative and dogmatic audience members whose predatorily comments cause you to revive your ambitions continuously.

Unlike a play at the theatre, many acts of life are impromptu and without a specific audience in mind. Therefore, you cannot always predict the audience members or their responses. However, information regarding potential audience members will be helpful.

Also, aside from theatre, the setting of the play and environment will help in the responses of the audience members. In my case, my accident occurred while performing a simple daily act experienced by all the audience members and myself. Walking up and down the stairs of a two-story house was as common as putting on pants. Therefore, to fall down those same stairs would equal, placing both legs in one pants leg. Ideally, this should not happen. Of course, I am over-simplifying the situation. Still, the point is, falling down the stairs set the stage for a passive response from the audience members due to the simplicity and commonality of the task and the audience members' perception. For instance, the audience members go up and down the stairs without accidents all the time. How does someone fall?

This is significant as having the leading role in your life. You need to be sure to control your performance. The stage and props you may not be able to control. However, your performance and reaction should reflect your real "character" and not influenced by the audience members' reactions or lack thereof. Self-control is the most crucial characteristic of the leading person in the story.

With social media allowing the world to seem closer to you with just the click of a finger, the opinion and reactions of others easily influence people. However, the only opinion that matters is yours. People will not do or say things that always meet your expectations, so you must be prepared to hear the unexpected and still be encouraged. This must come from the strength within. External influence should be limited, especially if it does not align with your aspirations.

VISION FROM THE GROUND

CHAPTER 14

TURN OPPOSITION INTO OPPORTUNITY

I am sitting on the stairs trying to gather myself, and I have this huge smile on my face, followed by a loud chuckle. This, however, is ironic, for I just fell. Shouldn't I be sad or disappointed? Those emotions never reached my mind. Instead, I found my situation and myself amusing. I am always one to review an event repeatedly in my mind to analyze where I went wrong. But, this time, I was inspired. The lessons discussed kept playing repeatedly. Rising from a fall, I begin writing this book—a perfect example of opposition, which turned into an opportunity and the first of many.

THE GREAT FALL

This notion is not new. Farther back when someone experienced a problem, being motivated to find a solution, inventions were created. Even in the same vein, we can address the misfortunes of life using the same concepts.

Another thing to note is that falls ignite creativity. So, do not get caught up in the negativity that trails your situation. Take the time out to fuss and show dismay. Get angry, be doubtful, or you can even cry. After giving the negativity life for a few hours, get over it, as you get busy with developing yourself and becoming better until you overcome. Use the fire that the opposition infused in you to ignite an opportunity. Definitely, an opportunity is out there if only you open your mind to a resolution.

As in my case, I had undergone my darkest moments before I rose in the dawn of my brightest days. As soon as I left my job, it seemed everybody else I knew experienced a financial crisis. Many people around me hit rock bottom, and there was a considerable need for help. Several cajoled me into helping out

TURN OPPOSITION INTO OPPORTUNITY

with their financial issues. Before I knew it, I was loaning money left and right. The case became that of an unemployed person loaning funds to employed individuals. How ironic? After the fifth loan, I was a little concerned and decided to keep tabs with my loaning limit. Despite my resolve, my sincere concern for family and friends who had valid financial needs won my budget over. Nevertheless, realistically, if anyone defaulted on the loan payment, I had no way to recover the funds, because I had no job or promising opportunity.

Indeed, my life took on a new direction when after a few months, an opportunity opened to me. I received the first loan repayment, and the person was grateful for the loan, that he repaid the loan amount in full, with an additional $100. The next person also repaid the loan amount in full and provided an additional $50. The trend of returning a little more than the loaned amount continued until all the loans got paid back. It was an exciting trend.

I not only received all my money back, but I received

THE GREAT FALL

"interest" additionally. Although the total "interest" received from the loaners was not quite significant enough to replace my income, it was more than the amount I would receive if I left the money in my bank account! Especially when checking and savings accounts provide interest rates of 0% and .09%, respectively.

The additional funds received challenged me to think of other creative ways to allow my money to create passive income above the .09% interest from my savings account. Driven by the new goal, I delved to research savings accounts that provided a higher interest percentage per year. I found two online savings accounts that fit the need: one providing 1.47% and another up to 2.5% interest annually. The interest rates were variable, but the possibility of increased funds was higher than my current savings account.

Moreover, one of the newly found savings accounts promoted a $600 reward when adding a new checking account. The reward was contingent on meeting spe-

TURN OPPOSITION INTO OPPORTUNITY

cific qualifications for 60 days after opening the account. I monitored the checking account to ensure that it met all qualifications.

While I remained unemployed, I was generating an income just by moving money around. My services included loaning money to people, and opening new savings and checking accounts. Now the money received was not a lot, but it only took me minutes to set up the accounts and transfer money to others or the banks. If I could place a timing on the number of hours I took to manage the accounts and loans, I invested no more than five hours.

Once I completed the initial set up, I had only a few more monitoring steps and automating transactions to finish. Therefore, if we took the additional funds received, about $750, divided by the time, which is five hours, then I made $150 per hour. Now that is a job I would not mind working! I still had to pay income taxes, but it was worth the time and effort.

THE GREAT FALL

The truth is opportunity hides in the opposition. You must see the potential and perform some research. Spend time locating resolutions or creative ways to implement a positive outlook in which you can benefit beyond your norm. Life is about growth, and that includes your outlook. The present way of doing things is not the only way; embrace newness.

CHAPTER 15

RENEWAL OF THE MIND

Two people can look at the same thing and view it differently. For example, a glass with a liquid that occupies half of the glass could be viewed as either half-empty or half full. Whether viewed as half-empty or half-full, only the perspective of the individual viewing the glass will determine which is correct.

When heading towards success, life's events occur to provide, develop, or renew our perspectives. Experiencing a fall provides the most exceptional insight on where you are, as the view from the bottom is whole, and provides clarity on how things are and not as they appear to be.

THE GREAT FALL

A perfect example is when you go through financial hardship. The friends you had before the hardship do not seem to be as reachable as they used to be, now that you need some assistance. You then realize that the individuals whom you thought were friends were merely convenient acquaintances only available when things were going great.

Maybe you unexpectedly lose your job, and in reviewing your savings account, you admit you have been living a financially irresponsible life. A fall can help you effectively assess where you are, here and now, as it relates to your goals and ambitions.

Friend, whenever you have an opportunity of rising back on your feet, do not be afraid to explore these opportunities. In your "Great Fall of Life" moments, reach out and embrace feasible chances that project themselves to you. Grab it, figure out how you will stand up again, and press forward.

Marrying the Great Divide: Work and Life

RENEWAL OF THE MIND

Your mind influences your lifestyle and decisions more than you can imagine. Your thought patterns, values, and principles affect the way you see and respond to different aspects of your life. In the workplace, everyone is seeking work-life balance. The dream is to find a job that will coincide with the other duties of life. I think it is ironic that society separated adult life into two categories: 'work' and 'life' when the phrase was coined.

For most people in society, it's almost as if work is not a typical function of life, such as getting married, having kids, receiving an education, or any other vital aspects of life. However, work is typically not optional and is essential for a person to survive. If a person does not work, then they do not eat. So, the question goes, "why is work separate from life? Is there such an idea as parent-adult balance?" I am sure several moms and dads want a brief separation between parenting and adulting; that is why babysitters are so loved.

THE GREAT FALL

With the "work-life balance" phrase alone, society has encouraged a mental divide between work and the other aspects of life. History has shown us that any intentional separation of items typically results in a perception of good versus evil or good and not so good. By default, since an average person enjoys having a family, learning, and so on, work would fall into the "not so good" category. On average, when asking someone about work, the response is not so chipper or happy. If you ask the same person about their kids, the reaction will be ultimately the opposite so much that you may have to convince them to discuss another topic.

But why does it have to be that way? I challenge you to alter your thinking. Instead of separating work from life, embrace work as a component of life. Doing this changes the way you feel about work, possibly minimizing the negative connotation. Additionally, you will naturally invest more effort into obtaining the job or career you desire or envision.

RENEWAL OF THE MIND

For instance, when your child does something they should not do, you will talk to them or punish them for illustrating the error of their ways. If you and your spouse are not seeing eye-to-eye, you may go to counseling. Even you may seek advice from a wise couple, purchase a lovely gift, or perform a task to improve the situation. If we could go to the extreme for any other aspect of life to foster a change in our favor, I believe we can do the same with our jobs or career. But why do we just complain when we should seek out ways out of our job challenges? Be just as happy and motivated at work as you are at home. And if you are not, strive for the change.

As my last words in this chapter, feel free to apply this principle to your faith as well. These characteristics are all aspects of you. In our life's pursuit, if no part of "you" must be jeopardized or compromised, then there must be a change! And the way onto this is to fight for a change in your perspective.

CHAPTER 16

INSPIRATION TO LIVE, MY WAY

After I fell, I quitted. I left my current job intending to live purposely and intentionally. I no longer desired to choose between my career, my health, my faith, and my family. Every aspect of my life was to complement each other. Since I was committed to my faith, my health, and my family, my career had to be flexible to align with the other three aspects of my life.

After four months of not looking for a job opportunity, I got hired by a company that met all my criteria. I became the Controller of a company with reasonable pay. I worked four days out of the week with the option to work from home. The owner and I shared similar faith and belief and stressed integrity

THE GREAT FALL

throughout all aspects of the company. I openly communicated my priorities and how this career move will play a part. I decided to no longer stress over my decisions to put my faith or family first. I am a wife and a mom first, and after seven years of being both, I am finally able to accept my roles without guilt.

Besides finding a fitting job, my fall altered my thoughts as it relates to the value I bring to the companies in which I work. Due to my vast work experiences, I did not question whether I can operate successfully in the position or meet the owner's expectations. My willingness to welcome new challenges in the past minimized all anxiety associated with the new job opportunity. With the new confidence, I launched an accounting consultation business simultaneously, having my first customer within a few weeks of initiation.

So, I fell with stress, anxiety, and confusion, only to rise on my faith and leading principles. I no longer fear losing a job. I am not worried about my career path. I know God has a plan for my life, and every event, whether positive or negative, is building characteristics for my future. I have a sense of peace regarding my career and hope others can share through adopting stated principles noted in this book.

My fall profoundly designed the life balance I desired.

Do not fall for a 'work-life' balance. Fall freely for your life.

About Author

I have always had a passion for finances and accounting. My mother, Linda, often told a story of how at the age of six years old, I once informed a grocery store cashier that she short-changed my mother by two cents. Astonished by my comment, the cashier asked, "what did that little girl say?" While holding the coins visible to the cashier, my mother replied, "she said you owe me two cents." After counting the coins, the cashier replied with a laugh, "I guess I do."

Looking back at the situation, I assume the cashier believed that there was no way that a little girl, who can barely see over the checkout counter, could accurately calculate the change that should be disbursed and compare the results to the coins that were actually provided in the short period of time. However, the cashier did not know that I enjoyed math and counting money. In fact, checkout was the best part of my grocery store experience as it allowed me to practice what I enjoyed doing and to see how much money my mom had in her possession.

I did not fully understand my calling at that time, but I grew to understand the validity of this story as I aged and increased by exposure to finances and accounting in high school and college. So, I graduated from college with the following degrees: Bachelor of Business Administration in Accounting and Master of Business Administration in Accounting.

Thereafter, I began my career working as an auditor for one of the "big four" public accounting firms. The knowledge and exposure I gained from my public accounting experience was priceless. I am forever grateful for the experience. After many years of auditing, I decided to experience the other side of accounting by switching to industry accounting with hopes of climbing up the corporate ladder

All my past experiences have challenged my thinking beyond my current view and have encouraged me to diversify my career. I am not only an accountant, but I am an entrepreneur in several different sectors including real estate and construction. Here is a secret: the foundation of operating a business is the same regardless of the product or service that is being sold. Once you learn the recipe, simply apply again and again.

www.ingramcontent.com/pod-product-compliance
Lightning Source LLC
LaVergne TN
LVHW051608070426
835507LV00021B/2825